Apocalypse
One Hundred

Apocalypse
One Hundred

Poems by

Richard Scarsbrook

TURNSTONE PRESS

Turnstone Press
Artspace Building
206-100 Arthur Street
Winnipeg, MB
R3B 1H3 Canada
www.TurnstonePress.com

MIX
Paper from
responsible sources
FSC® C004071

Turnstone Press gratefully acknowledges the assistance of the Canada Council for the Arts, the Manitoba Arts Council, the Government of Canada through the Canada Book Fund, and the Province of Manitoba through the Book Publishing Tax Credit and the Book Publisher Marketing Assistance Program.

Printed and bound in Canada.

Library and Archives Canada Cataloguing in Publication

Scarsbrook, Richard, author
Apocalypse one hundred / Richard Scarsbrook.

Poems.
Issued in print and electronic formats.
ISBN 978-0-88801-603-4 (softcover).--ISBN 978-0-88801-604-1 (EPUB).--ISBN 978-0-88801-605-8 (Kindle).--ISBN 978-0-88801-606-5 (PDF)

I. Title.

PS8587.C396A85 2017 C811'.54 C2016-908185-0
C2016-908186-9

This book is for Bluebell.

Contents

Apocalypse
One Hundred

Foreword

Disclaimer***

here's the pitch, strike two!
but wait, what's that
in the sky above the rim
of the bowl that holds us all?

let's raise our phones
and collectively record it, and
watch through our screens as these
united technologies

disjoin, divide,
disconnect, destroy

the general dynamics:

the rise and then fall

the
explosion, and then

disintegration,
and then

the extinction*

strike three! we're out
game over

but they had it coming, right?**

---

*mutually assured
**and so did we
***any rebroadcast, reproduction, or other use of the pictures and accounts of this incident without our express written consent is strictly prohibited

Unexpected Things Are Happening to Our Returning Astronauts

Urban Renewal

explosive charges roar
like a river after the thaw

the housing project cascades down
a waterfall of concrete dust

please disregard the tiny lives
that moved within these spaces

please clap your hands and cheer
as if it's Independence Day

the rocket's trail triumphant
until it bursts mid-stratosphere

the burning capsule spinning like an atom
please try not to think about its carbon nucleus

nothing to see here, folks
please move along

please continue to enjoy
your shopping day

like red cells in the bloodstream
the taillights flow along the highway

like shattered stars, the ashes
flutter back to earth

American Dream
(Clickbait #1)

I'm Wealthy. You're Not. *Click Here!*

6 Surprising Ways for
You
to Look Younger

Put
Your
blow-dryer on cold and make
Your
lotions do more

7 Ways to Land
Your
Dream Job

The best interview experiences
I've
had are where people ask
questions that
are kinda unique, like, "What's
Your
favourite movie?"

Is the Economic Downturn
Forcing
You
to Give Up
Your
Favourite Beauty products?

Among the downward
trends: cutting back
on styling gel and fragrance

I'm Rich. You're Not.

I
cracked the code to making
money
See How
I
Make
$3 Million Per Year!
You
Can Too

Click Here!

The Grim Reaper's Alphabet Song

alarm
boil water
coffee
drain cup
eventual clarity

fling towel
grab soap
hot water hissing

ignite engine
jammed traffic
killing you slowly

(let me out of here, please, you sigh)

money, chase money, but
none of your money can buy back the time
own the car and the house but your office owns you

please remit your payment in full and on time

quick now!
recite your Hail Marys
sing Hallelujah
the Lord is your Saviour
use your last breath
very soon you'll be done

wait for the
Xanax to still
your anxious heart

zero hour. . . too late

Unexpected Things Are Happening to Our Returning Astronauts
(Clickbait #2)

This stunning chandelier looks like a deep-sea creature!
Nylon stockings transformed into horrifying monsters!

A futuristic forest made from awesome laser beams!
OMG!

Colourfully cute monsters play their favourite cover songs!
Dazzling 3D chalk drawings will blow your mind!

Childhood photos of the world's most brutal dictators.
Sombre images from inside the wreckage of car crashes.

Too dark?

Hilarious images of cats dressed as pieces of sushi!
This outrageous car is made from 250 singing fish!

You have used 9 of your 10 free articles.
For unlimited access, click here to subscribe.

Unexpected things are happening to our returning astronauts.

Flying in an Armoured Rocket Suit

lately though
he no longer feels
as if he's moving at all
like he's a fixed point, and
it's the city that moves
around him

he watches his feet as
the sidewalk crawls
beneath them like a conveyor belt
then the twenty-first floor
brings itself
to him
through the elevator doors

sometimes he daydreams
he's swinging a light saber
flying in an armoured rocket suit
his alter-ego always gets the girl

but
not today
he can't
get his eyes to focus past
the shadow-eyed, pale-faced
stranger who
gazes back
absently
from the reflection
on the plexiglas
around
his six-by-six cubicle

Veteran

through the choking dust
air distorted by the heat
the screams and howls of the overwhelmed
a cacophony of shells
orders barked, cracking guns, thumping boots
through the blood-thick silences in between
he fights on

as metal pierces flesh
limbs are slashed, torsos skewered
eyes blinded, ears deafened
skins scorched
black and crimson
as his eyes burn like open wounds
he fights on

from beneath this crisp white sheet
fluorescent lights humming
a steady one-note dirge
this snake of clear tubing, hissing
into his parchment throat
pale, silent, withered
he fights on

put down your screen
and look at him

East Meets West
(Found in Translation)

America Flavour:
fresh life and delicious the street!

Napoleon fries the idea powder
have nice your college life!

butter many privates
funny toys come on together!

return to big nature feelings
your to see, I want face love!

instruction for the tourist:
advocate use civilization language

if you are stolen, call police immediate
obey the naughty palace safe navigation

infection disease, psychosis disease, stupid disease
any disease is forbid to here

forbid to carry sharp thing knifes
not permit to peer gunpoint with eyes

(archaeolinguists of the future
scratch your heads and wonder)

Do Not Disturb
tiny grass is dreaming

Alpha Dogs

Photoshop Mephisto

the sunlight plays on her candy-red toque
the ropes of her swing stretch heavenward

she smiles down upon a patchwork quilt
of tiny farms and clay-red roofs

you helped her fly, you placed her there
improved the beauty of her view

boosted the colour saturation
clicked her image into place

you have grown to love this woman
(although she's just a licensed photo)

but she belongs to you! so

aim that powerful wand of change!
slim and stretch her legs, and then

enlarge her breasts and head, so that
top-heavy, she tumbles, and

she can't get off the ground again

Treat Yourself!

the signs
burst through the haze of snow
as you drift north
on Yonge Street:

> Address your life!
> YONGE and RICH:
> EXPERIENCE LIVING at the centre of it all!
>
> STRONGER Body,
> STRONGER Swing.
> Golf Fitness Training: DOMINATE the course.
>
> Treat YOURSELF!
> GIFT and GET:
> Corporate Gifting Rewards Program.
>
> Feel the FREAK,
> Feel the FREEZE:
> When you drink Redline XTREME!
>
> TIME is MONEY!
> Express Lunch:
> Fifteen minutes or it's FREE

and then you see her, huddled
atop the steaming subway grate,
her message scratched in red
on a scavenged slice of cardboard:

> *I am homeless*
> *and I am hungry*
> *please help*

Speed Date
(Financial District Love Poem)

All hands on deck! Let's hit the ground running.
Let's drill down, and think outside the box.

Let's touch base. Let's take this offline. Ping me! Let's do lunch.

We can holistically coordinate our data, interactively utilize our synergy.

Let's unify our intellectual capital. We've got value-added fungibility.

We can formulate multimedia experiences,
implement forward-thinking technologies.

It's a no-brainer. It's so win-win. Bang for our buck! Let's get this ball rolling.

You're under water?
Don't have the bandwidth?
Your plate's already full?

At the end of the day, it's par for the course.

You can't win if you don't play.

Look at That Body
(Luminous Veil, Bloor Street Viaduct)

look at those eyes, pure Hollywood blue
(tinted contact lenses)

look at those straight, white, picket-fence teeth
(veneers and bleaching)

look at those pouting, rose-petal lips
(collagen needles, tattooed rouge)

look at those high, royal paycheque cheeks
(plastic fused to the bone)

look at those full, round, sculpted breasts
(skin-deep bags of silicone gel)

look at those abs, that Barbie-doll waist
(liposuction and starvation)

look at all that flesh, bone, and blood
(powder, plastic, and dye)

found
splattered on the
rock-hard
riverbed mud

next year they will erect
the luminous veil
a suicide prevention measure

an eyesore, folks will say

Five Minute Break

she's not the uniform
or the name tag, she
doesn't glow like
the neon sign outside, she's
not from the bygone era claimed
by Betty's Rest Stop Diner

on break she sits outside, atop
a picnic table, just
to get away from you all, the
morning air cool and fresh
like a handful
of melting ice

soon another wave will roll on in
trucks full of men, they
will call her baby, whistle
as she walks away

and this moment
trickles through
her fingers before she
can plan
her escape

so she limps back inside
into the stagnant, greasy air

Alpha Dogs

throw your meat to the dogs who snarl
who bare their perfect teeth

stroke their sleek, black suits
reward their barks, their greedy whines

toss them toys and rub their chins
unseal your tins of wet rewards

and to the dog that licks your hand
wag your finger, say:
good dog, faithful dog
you'll get your reward soon

but the dog that licks
is hungry now
he leaps the fence
escapes the cage

to run

to hunt

to eat

and barking, snarling, pissing
the pack moves on

for now your toys are broken, your
empty tins roll on the floor

Fortress

you had them build your walls so tall
that nobody could scale them

you had them build your walls so thick
nothing could penetrate

your foundations are so deep that no
one could ever dig you out

the strongest steel and stone were used
no expense was spared

and the single door that you designed
opens only from the inside

and you've camouflaged your fortress
so that it cannot be seen

you have everything you need
except for one essential thing

and from deep inside your soundproof room
you cry from underground:

discover me
free me
find a way inside

It Rained Down from Above

from six feet above them
you
preached the abstract
converted the mundane
into monuments
of truth
your cool blue jacket rippling
in the onstage Freon wind

and from six feet below
they
were held spellbound
their bodies swaying in an ocean
of five thousand believers
arms flailing above
their hot glowing bodies
their fingers licking the sky
like fickle tips of flame

you drank from their thirst
and chilled in their heat
your view from the stage
like a pilot's view of a fire

and when your words
like water
pounded down

they all believed
their lives would be saved

Emergency Broadcast System

The Impressionists

a slim tapered brush dipped in Napthol Scarlet
could depict the distracted arcs of her lips

a single straight stroke from course flat bristles
for the Coal Black mane she's just untied

but you're too absorbed
to reach for a brush

the tympanic rumble that rattles
the windows
is erased by the rhythmic rushes of blood
in your eardrums and in hers

a sepia-tinted monochrome print
could freeze the devouring cloud's approach

but she is too far gone
to reach for a camera

alas, there is nothing that you can do
but come together once again
as the city disintegrates

Nightmare
(Monday Morning, 3 AM)

airborne, soaring
the fall in reverse
heavy and knotted, waterlogged limbs

bound like a mummy
can't scratch, can't move
fade out
fight back
fade out again

it's a bad one
wow
worst I've seen
my God

throat like a scab
panicked tongue probes
no teeth, no jaw
can't swallow, can't speak

patient's conscious
put him under
quick now
quick

a sound like an endless dry heave
the wail of a mournful ghost
it's you
that's your voice, son

tag him, man
write him down as gone
this one isn't
coming back

this is not
what they said it would be

Scan Button
(Evacuation Traffic Jam)

they all heard the prophecy
and had the same idea:

get out, get away
stomp the pedal to the floor

put it in the rearview mirror
before the clocks hit zero

now the line of cars stretches
to the heat-blurred horizon

the overheated hissing
of failed radiators

traffic twisted and inert
a snake baking in the sun

to drown the dissonant chorus
of frustrated horns

all you can do
is roll up the window

crank the A/C
until the fuel runs out

and punch the SCAN button,
searching for the song

perfect for the moment
when the final credits roll

Number One Hit
(on YOU 95.7 FM this week)

In the spaces
between our ears, behind our faces
are the things in which we trust
instead of what's in front of us

But still we try
to keep everything inside
though we're bursting at the seams
filled with unrequited dreams

From our bedrooms
we post links up in the chat rooms
hoping that they'll see the signs
that we hid between the lines

Our decisions are undemocratic
Our opinions are problematic
Our delusions are hyperdramatic
Our conditions are psychosomatic

We're Complicated Boys
We're Complicated Girls
Wooo-oooh, oh woah woah
We're complicated

No one ever listens to the lyrics, though.

Emergency Broadcast System

it always began:

This
is a test.
For the next sixty seconds, this
station will conduct
a test
of the Emergency
Broadcast System.
This is only
a test.

then:

that tone
that shrillpiercing skinspeckling heart-
stopping tone
that frequency, screeching:

thebombswillbefallingsoon!
yourskinwillbeliquified!
yourboneswillexplodeintoash!

boy, you will never
touch the flesh of a woman

you will never
know true love

then:

Broadcasters, in
cooperation with the FCC and
other authorities, have
developed this system
to keep you informed
in the event
of an actual emergency.

now:

you miss that familiar frequency
as the crackling radio static

matches the fire in the sky

these streets I wander
alone but still together
sidewalks glazed with rain

framing reflections
photographing places I
wish that we could share

if I became dust
wouldn't your nostrils and lips
breathe me into you?

into your lungs, I'd
mingle with your particles
sublimate, diffuse?

that glow on your skin
the taste of salt, that Bordeaux
blush around your mouth

that mixture of tongues
absorb that jungle-wild scent
the steam of our heat

mix me a drink with
a taste that makes me as drunk
as desire is deep

surround me, rushing
this shivering feeling like
learning how to swim

Penny Wishes

break the water's skin and sink
like a lucky penny thrown
into a wishing fountain

your body will
spiral down

spiral down

spiral down

blood warm water will fill your ears
with the gurgling rush of waves through sand
you'll be almost sleeping

almost dreaming

ebb and flow

ebb and flow

ebb and flow

break up through
the water's rippled skin
like the penny's rising wish

your body will

spiral up

spiral up

spiral up

blood fills your ears, sea-water warm
nothing has been extinguished
the fire still burns, outside you

and inside you

ebb and flow,

ebb and

and

Roar and Trickle

a roaring roll of thunder
tumbling bright through smoky clouds

this crisp white linen sacrificed
to rolling writhing love

the rumbling echo swallows
our mutual ritual cries

gasp in recognition
and then it's lost, then it is gone

the universe collapses
we knew that this day would come

but is there a patter of raindrops?
is there a flutter of curtains?

are we gone or has existence
merely left us both behind?

a flash of light
that no one sees

and a rush of wind
that no one hears

and here upon
our window

the water pools
and trickles down

Event Horizon

Decomposition
(The Dead Sea Scrolls)

preserved for our reverence
in air-tight cases
under filtered light
motion sensors
hovering guards

brown and ragged-edged
these scraps of Genesis
like dead islands from the air
fragments reassembled
continental drift in reverse

The Covenant of Damascus
with instructions to the exiles
on what to do with lepers
how to keep them from the tribe
how to keep the faithful pure

written right to left
these psalms on leather
nearly turned to earth
Bless, O my soul,
The LORD

on the finely wrought parchment
with script clear and bold
The Book of War
survives the ages
better than the rest

The Academy Award for Best Cinematography

remember that shot of the airplane, though?

that orange-red-violet sunset spectrum
reflected on its mirror-silver skin, its
turning twin propellers like the promise of a future?

and the black reality of the airstrip, which
sliced the screen from corner to corner, like
a threat, like a reminder?

wasn't that lovely?
wasn't that something?
wasn't it?

of course, the critics
concentrated on
the dialogue, which they called stilted
the acting, overwrought
the scenes, overlong
the resolution, incomplete
the swelling strings of the soundtrack, obvious and overstated

but that tracking shot

of that plane going down

was really

really

something

wasn't it?

Blaze of Glory

our elders always pictured it
as hellfire raining down

the wrath of one appalled
by we ungrateful brats

who imagine it done Hollywood
in bigscreen aspect ratio

drumroll of machinegun fire
prelude to the mushroom clouds

rumbling in Dolby Surround
please leave your 3D glasses here

but did it begin
with Jenny on Oprah

vaccinations waning
demons springing back to life?

or was it
when you teased

the dragon's chlorofluorocarbon breath

on the hottest day of the century?

it's a mere sickened wheeze
this final wilting of the
withered

it's not the blaze of glory
that we were waiting for

Making the Call

heart murmurs, weakness
(in the body, in the legs)

involuntary oscillation
(the rolling of the eyeballs)

the confusion and circling
disorientation

dilated pupils, retinal detachment
a subconjunctival hemorrhage

blood in the urine
bleeding from the nose

at this point, it's all about the quality of life
comfort, silence, dulling the pain

here's special food, a special bed,
a special, easy-access box

drugs to ease the agitated mind, to numb
the fight or flight response

but is it too late? are we too far gone?
is it time to let us go?

the doctor fills the needle
with Ketamine
and waits

Behind the Glass

and then there's darkness
the pop of revolutionary pistols

it's on our speakers
we shake our heads and change the channel

we're good Christians
Jews and Muslims
Buddhists
Agnostics, Atheists
and some of us check the
Other box

and the thing we all believe is that
it will stay right there behind the glass

like a museum diorama of The Crusades, or
a collage about The War to End All Wars

but then there's darkness
the rat-a-tat-tat-tat of automatic weapons

it's coming from outside our windows
we place our fingers on our lips, and then our hands in the air

Event Horizon
(The Big Crunch)

the golden age ungilded
the great leap backward
one by one, the satellites
vanished from the sky

the greatest generation
shrank into embryos
the moon moved six feet
closer to the earth

only the birds did the tweeting
only the bees produced the buzz
lasers, bar codes, microchips,
robotics: meaningless

no credit cards, synthetics,
supermodels, superglue
five billion fewer humans
a million species resurrected

and at the moment that
the universe began
contracting into
a black hole singularity

from which no light
nor sound
nor hope would ever
escape

the last fertile human being took a selfie with its phone

Civilized
(Revisionist History)

This will be your cube. It measures ten by ten.

Just like every other cube, for equality and fairness.

You will not exceed the limits. You will not fall behind.

You will meet your targets daily, precisely, and exactly.

You will not complain. You will not criticize.

You will respect your coworkers, and obey your superiors.

You've got a mortgage to pay, and debts to abate.

Please be punctual, but please do not loiter.

Please be restrained. Please be civilized.

What
the fuck?

Where
do you think
you're going?

There is
nowhere
but here!

Who
do you think
you are?

Afterword

Milque not Milk

shadow-eyed and pale-faced
should be counted as two words each
not one

my
Word's worth more
than Microsoft's

and shrillpiercing skinspeckling heartstopping?
that's clearly six, not three

I
don't even need my MFA
to spot those missing spaces
                    (the interviewer listens to you
                    and twists the camera lens)

I
punch closer to the knuckle than
those other milquetoasts dare!

(and, yes, it's milque, not milk)

I
will rubber-stamp this assemblage:
minimizereducedismiss
                    (for the interviewer's single reflex
                    you squint so manfully

                    and ironically, too, because, you know,
                    the glasses)

Clark Kent into Superman!
Protecting the Canon!
Vanquishing Opponents!

(with blog posts)

Notes

"Disclaimer***" mentions by name two of the most profitable arms manufacturers in the world, while also paraphrasing one of the world's most famous disclaimers.

"American Dream" was created from direct quotes from the front pages of the Yahoo and MSN "news" websites on US Independence Day, 2009.

"Unexpected Things Are Happening to Our Returning Astronauts" was created from headlines that appeared on an internet "News Feed" during January 2014.

"East Meets West (*Found in Translation*)" was created from the English translations printed on various Chinese, Japanese, Korean, and Taiwanese products, menus, and signs.

About the title of "Photoshop Mephisto": One literal translation of "Mephisto" (from Hebrew) is "falsehood plasterer."

The Luminous Veil (from "Look at That Body") is an anti-suicide barrier that was erected on Toronto's Bloor Viaduct. It is estimated that up to 500 people had leaped from the viaduct between the viaduct's opening in 1918 to the completion of the barrier in 2003.

The Emergency Broadcast System was an emergency warning system, utilizing local radio and television stations, which was used from 1963 to 1997.

"Decomposition" was inspired by the exhibition "Dead Sea Scrolls: Words that Changed the World" at the Royal Ontario Museum, Toronto, January 2010.

And, yes, every poem in this collection contains exactly one hundred words (as verified by the "Word Count" function built into Microsoft Word).

Acknowledgements

A prose version of the poems “Event Horizon *(The Big Crunch)*” and “Blaze of Glory” called “Blaze of Glory *(The Big Crunch)*” was a finalist for the inaugural Bath Flash Fiction Award, 2015.

A prose version of “Emergency Broadcast System” was also long-listed for the prize noted above, also in 2015.

“Emergency Broadcast System” was published in the *Scrivener Creative Review* in Spring 2015.

“Alpha Dogs” was published as “Team Alpha Male T-Shirts” in *The Stockholm Review of Literature* in September 2014.

“Roar and Trickle” appeared in the September 2014 edition of *The Steel Chisel.*

“Haiku for the Ravenous” was short-listed for the Ireland-based 2013 Fish Poetry Prize.

Part of “Haiku for the Ravenous” was published in the anthology *Haiku for Lovers* (Buttontapper Press, 2013).

“Look at That Body” was published in *Vallum* 9:2, “Urban Landscapes / Hidden City” Spring/Summer 2012.

“The Grim Reaper’s Alphabet Song” and “Flying in an Armoured Rocket Suit” (then called “Secretary”) were published in March 2004 in *Carousel* (Vol. 15).

“The Grim Reaper’s Alphabet Song” also appeared in *O2: Coming Up For Air,* Cranberry Tree Press, 2002.

“Veteran” appeared as "Veterans' Hospital" in *Witness: anthology of war poetry* (Serengeti Press, 2004).

“It Rained Down from Above” was published as “Icon” in *The Saving Bannister* anthology (Canadian Authors Association, 2003).

Most of the poems noted above were published in slightly to significantly different forms.

Gratitude

I worked on some of the poems in this book during my term as Writer in Residence at the North York Central Library (Fall 2014). Thank you to Greg Kelner and the Toronto Public Library for the rewarding opportunity to assist the public with their writing projects while also developing my own.

My thanks once again to Turnstone Press for publishing this, my second volume of poetry, my third book with Turnstone, and my ninth book overall.

My most heartfelt gratitude goes to poetry editor extraordinaire Sharon Caseburg, whose thoughtful and incisive guidance was once again invaluable!

For their abundant love, support, and encouragement, my thanks as always to my wonderful family, especially my parents, Mike and Judy Scarsbrook.

Thanks to my many loyal friends. To once again paraphrase Bill Murray, "Be careful who you choose as your friends. I'd rather have four quarters than a hundred pennies." My pockets are full of silver dollars, and I am always grateful.

And, as always, this book is for Bluebell. Thank you for your love.